Customer proposes, business disposes, competition opposes

Market power rules

Poleman Robb

CV Madhavi

C Rajgopal

High value low risk

- The exercise does simple task of Customer terms with higher ideal for your business risk of manageable proportions so that employees get new more from traditional less for lessons dying as values of life get replaced by advanced, selfish and hollow expenses.

Competition is not ally

- With all collaboration and partnerships in business globally competitive responses should not be questioned by agreement and laws because they are the direct forces of spontaneity and natural sequences of industrial evolution.

Customer proposes

- No price pressure on performance pressure
- Green environment before making gadgets
- Tight focus on money for her satisfaction but not seller's
- Contradictory platforms to be provided with your business success.

Contradictory platforms

- Customer wants low-cost and change is high-priced performance management
- Market has competition and still has concurrent price, features and Strategy
- Leadership advantages, players, spots, mediums, risks and consideration goals are all different many but clarity is none with business as one with customers.

Business disposes

- Of corrections in lieu of time and money
- Of completion in lieu of competition
- Of its brand in line with consumer esteem
- Of lies in top quality technology in multiple ways of improving community
- The last two are good yield business changes
- The first two side Business shutdown

Competition opposes

- The beginning itself as great business expectations touch grounds of Customer dreams
- Exquisite attempts to be Customer's apple of eyes only to cover with goggle of business rivalry exploitation

Business double

- Knowledge has skills of avoiding penalties
- Experience the best to become the best and create the best
- Technology and men cannot do away with each other
- Sales and losses go hand in hand

Current decision

- Firms in struggle with customers and employee teams could possibly propose solutions routed through users and makers should the decision be stuck if left to top bosses and then commit your business success to hiring best, training worst, understanding most of the customer groups interacting with employees.

Flowchain

- Flowchart illustrates a common flow model
- Flow chain is for inclusion of multiple classes of business changes and responsibilities of tasks and stakeholders because business is designed with entirety of Customer as your business beneficiary of paid solutions. The goal of Customer- the business needs - resources allocation- assessment - action points- results - reviews - lessons.

Strategic position

- Never deviate from Customer
- Never put Customer as your caretaker, follower and defaulter
- Though Customer is business stakeholder she has no stake in business losses but company has stake in customer satisfaction levels.

User proposal

- Is a bid to try and firm up new vistas of business changes with knowledge of different companies but finally meeting the needs of Customer in the best possible way of collaboration between customers and employees.

Technology proposal

- Ethics and employees should have more tries with men before granting control to machine that is icy in customer interaction with soft and hard forms of technology that could give customers price justified solutions but value can really come from nowhere but human contribution.

Technology disposal

- There's no fully automatic in the real sense without any user interface at complete machine for zero human intervention that goes along development, testing, repair or man trying to understand machine (not without random behaviour).

Technology opposition

- Is there any automation to detect undue influence of men on machine or code (not bugs) to get sensors on for your skill when needed? Grand ultra tech work for your business success by saving overall cost at optimisation of operations development custom of planned solutions Strategy.

Supposition

- The goal of Customer is free products when she would pay most for new products made to her wholesomeness
- Customer is no lone star but has responsibility of family
- Tell the customer to give you a ear, tell employees to give you a resignation.

Market power imposes

- Surrender of business players to fundamentals
- Competition of Price-product disparity between old and new business firms
- Up trends in innovation but not without incremental risk of change

Market power poses

- Political implications for new government punchlines arise out of business imbalances brought by external environment wants.
- Stable market shares hidden Power to get rivals to display winning tactics.
- Like that bird market feeds randomly and flies far to get new importance.

Market power dozes on

- Active Brand followers
- agile business changes
- Temporary success factors affecting business reality unless we work with facts and chaos alike
- Leaders who can help customers even at the cost of slight.

Market closes on

- Cultural variations of business and Customer give good time to market for throwing challenges and players in different directions but volatility of market lets it remain unclear or hidden in the myriad of business ideas.

Business loses on

- Technology gaps
- Investment expectations
- Customer feedback
- Research utilisation
- Innovation differential

- The above are inevitable business failure losses.

Economy poses for

- Monetary and fiscal measures alter the business by economic twists and turns to get market signals altered in multiple ways that you as Customer can't fathom under volatility but time normalisation is impending in such transition time.

Market snoozes

- On certain rival activity that is trying to satisfy market imbalance due to which market bounces on new opportunities for connecting with volatility
- When we represent the process and not Customers, to leave Companies carry out the mutual biases to get haphazard results from equally weird response.

Market harmony

- Comes when buyers, sellers, dealers, advisors, stakeholders and others act as quick gain makers in different directions with your future prospects in the same goal of growth and commitment to your immediate dependents.

Industrial cacophony

- Customer opposes the opportunities exploited by companies but market gets excited
- The changes can grow you to stagnant industry so that Customers change to pick from your business leftover, cdman and instant photography went back to old methods for nod.

Melody of Customer

- Competition should not be allowed to understand your customers unless you have weak employees who can not rejoice interference and criticism of Customer as a dramatic business tonesetter.

Market tosses

- Trends changing Companies belief that modify response
- Product innovation and variety of no value addition but degrading Customer cultures
- Knowledge and skills to get them flying in profit
- Technology failure to pay for human slavery in surfdom.

Industry Moses

- Experts in Practices
- Advisors of business changes
- Theorists in customer service
- Strategists of Customer delight
- Maintenance providers and repair supporters to get multiple technical formalities in constant change.

On user noses

- Let Customer boss around poking nose in business administration with your future prospects coming wherever not expected
- Let not anger sit on Customer nose by risking of it getting worse
- Let your business credibility be part of Customer pride .

Technology roses

- Manufactured intelligence is no luxury or basic help with thorns of Customer volatilities that seek functions beyond novelties of logic from man to machineries running in customer service and support from start through competition as indicators of individual productivity or efficiency.

Collective competition

- Bargaining is akin to customers and responsibilities are rewarded for employees to identify different possibilities of competition and collaboration with the global attempt of future Innovation for satisfaction of Customer as a business tool for new change initiatives.

Responding to change

- Follow Customer as change driver
- Observe Companies as your culture mirror
- Reverse failure to get it back in change
- Attach capital to change returns
- Invite Customer as your change manager
- Invest time with the global economy change

Predicting change

- Track your company and Customers' feedback
- Transfer resources and benefits for next moves
- Transform business with development in favour of Customer
- Train employees to enable them return the best for new change.

Product roars

- The changes in culture of Customer
- The business culture and ethics
- The rival tactics and employees' dedication
- The market and community gains
- Are captured, considered, controlled or catered by products.

Customer bosses

- The market is first boss and business representatives must take into account to be in the habit of services in respect of Customer as your culture with treating your duty as your hobby or fun in providing specific hiqual outputs to improve your business impression on Customer perceptions.

Process closes

- Business process closes on your customer to eliminate any ambiguity and give specific customised care or commitment including greater satisfaction of getting business significance of opportunities to understand Customer and community.

Optimisation tosses

- Utilisation gap and Customer understanding are tossed with various attempts on optimisation aiming for new efficiencies and benefits in business globally for competitive development through coexistence of the business stakeholders and technology infrastructures.

Operations lose

- Efficiency falls in the process of establishing superiority of Customer over Business innovation in employees and technology with competition aligning gaps in complete favour of user or seller by nurturing openness, learning and trust in the same business market that is working with different goals for money and Innovation.

Market truce

- Industrial and Customer collaboration in the best interests of the backward section of the society will go with market as new riskfree business changes with no other side-effects of market information completely ignored in the growth cause of strengthening global community.

Rivals use

- Your good cultural skills to help customers think that they could swing in for rivals who can grow better than your business products, so your customer information on personal managerial attention to change product as per customisation demand can bring better deal.

Tactics amuse

- Competition is now slowly working in improving your business products or their experimental results in adjusting Strategy with your business response stead by playoffs and reactions of cultural relevance to buyer who still values that emotional connect in customer service and product promotion tactics of companies.

Strategy muses in customer

- Though the management teams look at the formulation and implementation to be useful to employees, the overall process and value originate in customer satisfaction by not losing their cultural importance or inner delight in product expectations.

Analyse and apprise

- Get help and influence of Customer in future discussion of business products in general analysis following which you should apprise of Customer in future expectations

Deviation accuses

- Customer of less quality or exaggerated feedback
- Product of lacking innovation
- Process of lacking integration

Total cost management

- The changes, new business opportunity, different types of growth as won over rivals should be balanced with positive Strategic response by reducing the cost

Innovation fuses

- Ideas and needs
- Technology and knowledge
- Total experience and skills transformation of business products improving their user state of activity

Business host

- Customer is a guest in business
- Businesses bring hospitality of products
- Product is not exclusively made by companies but as helpful collaboration with customers

Cure or procure

- Cure the process and operations deviation or procure the latest technology that goes into default fixing of gaps
- Cure the market threats and procure the latest knowledge that go on employee training and enrichment of business products.

Influence on technology

- Customisation in business Technology occurs due to man-made reason not to uplift market power or Business efforts but to satisfy top management inhibition of adjustments in line with their inconvenience or selfishness.

Skill grows

- Knowledge has a reason for getting skill and tool applied in better way to be influenced by the two in return for skills can add to Knowledge by discovery of advanced methods for optimum performance.

Deep Strategy

- Delve into deeper challenges of application of knowledge and skills to get new impact of market transitions and business strategy by controlling competitors for addressing genuinely buyer needs more on excellence than other forms of business opportunities.

Measured tactics

- The market and Customer as your desired Business drivers from the internal process and environmental inputs to get the right outputs on expectations of users with information dissemination done in market demand tactics to support measured progress without affecting the performance.

Competition as

- Base for Customer interaction could give you a new but less brand uniqueness ever increasing international rivalry with quality, risk, credibility by the same level that should be able to respond on Customer worth

Risk Strategy

- The company should show its ideas, planning and business opportunities for analysis by experts in delving into the process deviations, loopholes or other business information risks to be hindrance in the business and Customer tactics.

Business gaps

- Seal the process deviations and employee lacunae in business learning and corporate management value by giving more innovative and creative cultural skills to handle the market and Customer satisfaction.

User chooses

- Technology over traditional methods with the hope of improving the values by the saving made in Technology offering as a better solution for your present need.
- The changes in culture and fashion of accommodation for new products that help with different types of strength like safety, networks and convenience of users.

Rivals impose

- Risk of experiments and reaction in business globally to get multiple losses inflicted on your business on losing the spontaneity of Customer interaction when you want to stay competitive and connected with Strategic planning for magnifying experience benefits for your business credibility.

Social networks boast of

- Go ahead with the global business development that aims at different levels of learning and progress on the social development through user growth by combining resources and information to get multiple common contextual factors addressed.

Market dozes

- On ignorance of business with understanding and interpretation of market signals, Companies can lose their track and use by Customer who has ability to watch or influence their market for reaction in sentiment or direction.

Innovation diagnoses

- The market improvement or upliftment scopes for Customer value to verify your submission in Technology to sort gaps in social efficiency of learning from the product in how to use machine learning and usage experience at the achievement of Customer growth.

Stakeholder poses

- To be taken in stride of Customer advocate and market representative at different levels of investment, employments, development, participation and contribution to your business success but market or Customers have no replacement or representations except for direct involvement..

Investors toss

- Big business stakes are not in a investment returns hike or risk management but opportunities exploring market sentiments of paying more attention to Customer needs and upliftment.

Resources source

- Skills
- Knowledge
- Experience
- Strategic adaptation
- Outputs of certain quality and value

Demand blooms

- With competitive Innovation in the space of compliance and community development at two ends of the process initiatives
- Within your business investment in customer satisfaction levels even at different levels of product quality

Common zones

- Customer and employees are dependent upon the market value more than modern technology to receive higher levels of business performance and productivity gains.

Lopsided development

- The changes that need your skill and tool for Customer satisfaction could close on perfect business or asymmetrical development of business with the different factors affecting inputs and outputs so train your employees to get long-term insight into future Innovation.

Balanced budget

- Management of Customer product or technology services to provide highest financial planning quality of retaining expenses or profits without compromising on the variance limits and Customer expectations.

More useful products

- Employees are human assets, Customer is fixed asset with no depreciation and limitations but are permanent opportunities for growth of your products which are not always useful or selling against other companies.

Native Innovation

- Local product or technology innovations could not be ignored because they deserve to perform in multinational environmental protection of base, internal environment, external markets and the objective of improving community on various domains.

Rated by

- Middle to start for relevant positions because anyway it's a new chapter open in Innovation up the market path of completely different products
- Highest to pathbreaking for your customer interaction by account of interference and feedback.

Haggling toggle

- The company knows that solutions for Customer need to defer the market leader on preferences of different business products or abilities of toggling in Technologies to haggle for best results.

Demanding unexpected

- The company to employees and customers to companies
- Sometimes market may turn demanding to customers
- Could be a new business opportunity or failure.

Optional mistake

- It's better to commit mistakes than avoiding in learning and thinking of the business stakeholders and their advantage immediately flowing through technology and corrections as services to help with the options of blaming on technology and training in skills; blaming on the learning curve and moving forth.

Customer is

- Life of business
- Employees should think dynamic about Customer as friend in need
- Stakeholders are great guys as long as Customer demands something.

Business is

- Source of Customer service
- Journey of solutions excellence
- Destination of each employee expectations
- Medium of communication and collaboration in growing economies

Research is

- Happening for your skill of aligning Business to fresh world of actions putting social change at first to get new relevance of information
- Required for your business credibility or capabilities as recognition of hardworking unit firm and not superficial participation in customer service.

Power embraces

- Market when it becomes mandatory path and source of opportunities and competition in reducing tactical friction
- Customer when they have to work for new change within your business products
- Company when they have a good attempt of delighting Customer.

Expand their contribution

- Help Business user enhance their skill or contribution increasing international quality of your products which can never win by being considered independent of Customer experience, usage and expectations.

14 Ms

- Men, management
- Mentor, milestones
- Machine, measures
- Money, masteries in skills and knowledge
- Material, mission
- Mettle, mistakes to learn
- Methodology
- Marketing

8 C categories

- Current scenarios
- Cultural affiliation
- Customer experience
- Company focus
- Competition Strategy
- Capabilities management
- Community outreach
- Cooperative collaboration

7 T- phrases

- Trouble shooting
- Technology multiplicity
- Tested testimonials from Customer
- Tactical leadership gear
- Trained talent pool
- Top management quality
- Team execution excellence

Dynamic Technology chooses

- Dependency on patents and Customer satisfaction grills business with distinct excellence from the two sides of Technological or community preferences on providing intelligence Innovation and not skeletal Innovation without creating future success path.

Customers

- Compose business changes with tunes for better future solutions
- Users are composed by the different products expectations, experience and dreams of getting pampered by competition.

Rivals

- Pose challenge for churning out more ways of standardisation of business solutions that are limiting the scope of Customer influence and user demands on the market because companies can get better say then.

Market research

- Tosses in business options with customer cultural values of global change can get you different types of ideas in futuristic growth strategies for investment by users and business representatives.

Dash of business

- Competition is not a problem when companies can grow trained user and staff collaboration onvalues and skills to handle technologies and culture of getting products aligned with trust instead of competition response wars.

Tough market

- Market has power but company interpretation and business changes against signals alter the market path on making it sound, tough, twisty or simple for your business innovation to roll around unutilised capacities to get multiple things done in the pursuit of success.

Trained by Customers

- Market becomes mandatory path on which you could depend on information on competition as trained by Customer who wants something different from each player in business knowledge of customer service.

Useful times

- Features comparisons
- Financial control
- First competitive response
- Fair cost
- Fine conditions of market

Technology loses

- Though amazing for your youth Technology loses confidence of global buyer on values and ethos building trust between provider and Customer that you have to reinstate by allowing human intervention in some form or other.

Market is not

- A win for new change always
- A road of roses to pickup Colors of your choice
- A door to opportunities for every company
- A combination of weak and winning competitor but sometimes itself becomes stagnant.

Competitive nos

- Compete not without incremental gains of user, in business solutions that differ by price, utility, features or other forms of Customer acceptance because they are deciders of your business credibility or market standing.

Influence on

- Market can come from two different types- Innovation in business and user trends changing investment gains
- Competition is due to man-made reason for war on buyers without quality success

Everything else

- Capabilities are your plans into turning real of Customer expectations in rewarding them more than modern experience and successful lifestyle skills from usage of technology that goes into management of your products. Everything else is needed in business and user favour on enabling future prospects in connection with market success.

Competition

- Bets on your customer care or your business credibility in gaining some extra share of slips
- Beats the market path of business changes by working with other things on competitive adaptation of players' strategy.

Piloting for Customer

- Companies fly free on Customer dreams to give more tangible useful products that help customers with no harm effects on the daily improvement effort in market that is formless without Customer information how much ever irrelevant.

Time to market

- Depends upon identification of time fit for competitive retardation in market after working with customers on different types of ideas in identifying the right needs.

Let Customer understand

- Don't overproduce for extracting more gains from Customer
- True Business leader should definitely try to reduce risk and burden of Customer in saving more resources on redundant gaps that multiply the needs.

Be responsible

- Don't cheat Customer by giving new output as product variety hiding behind commonality in competition or market overcommitment or other information juggling facts and confusion together.

Helpless Customer

- Don't bring the customer to say - ok take whatever it costs, have your terms and give me whatever but let's close and come free as early as possible. Let me get rid of you as soon as possible.

www.ingramcontent.com/pod-product-compliance
Lightning Source LLC
Chambersburg PA
CBHW020553220526
45463CB00006B/2283